Flights of Nature

Reflections on Kent's North Downs.

2019-2021

Maryanne Grant Traylen

Modern History Press

Ann Arbor, MI

Flights of Nature: Reflections on Kent's North Downs (2019-2021)

ISBN 979-8-89656-105-7 paperback
ISBN 979-8-89656-106-4 hardcover
ISBN 979-8-89656-107-1 eBook

Published by
Modern History Press
5145 Pontiac Trail
Ann Arbor, MI 48105
Phone +1 734 417 4266
Fax +1 734 663 6861
info@modernhistorypress.com

Distributed by Ingram Book Group (USA, UK, EU, AU, CA)

UK retailers: please visit this link to order or sign up
https://LP.ingramcontent.com/publishers/uk-wholesale

Contents

Introduction

The act of recording what makes up a particular moment—birdsong, trees, sun and clouds—is more than just an assembling of scenic elements. It's a way of saying something timeless and urgent: do away with the not-here, this is what there is, the simple intensity of being alive.[1]

How an ordinary dog-walker can soar, *Flights of Nature* describes the inspiration gleaned from the season-changing richness of Down, vale, sea and sky, simple landscapes available to all. Like its prequel *Ring of Downs, Flights of Nature* takes its cue from the area around East Kent's North Downs Way. That is the circle whose northeastern and southeastern arcs lead through Canterbury and the Folkestone Downs respectively. The mandala which in Sanskrit denotes circle, cosmos or divine abode. *Flights of Nature* takes the months of the year as its format and circle in time. The ellipse is the year.

Starting here, for everywhere, sentient land offers itself up as fodder for reflection, flexing our feelings with energy and wonder. Our thoughts with challenge and solace.

Land as flesh sharpens. Joy drops to earth. Like seeds to be sunk into fertile soil, our airborne thoughts long to land too, grounded, unlike flights of fancy, in flights of nature. Mind by matter. Up by down. High by low. Two in one.

Once, long ago, Platonic then Cartesian dualism separated these opposites and made an association that however unconsciously, sank deep into our western psyches. Of a masculine 'spirit' superior to a feminine 'matter'. Fostering an attitude that gave reason to seek mastery over matter. Plunder Mother Earth until she could hardly breathe.

Flights of nature as opposed to its emptier counterpart in flights of fancy, are full within us as we walk through forest or field, along shore or clifftop; nourished and focused, our

---

[1] Philip Marsden, *The Summer Isles*, Granta 2020, p. 214

moving body combining flesh with spirit; the overcoming of divisions enabling us to take mental 'flight'. Outside where there is odour, sight and sound, scents spawn into fresh air, pheromones rise from soil, flowers burst from their buds, grass susurrates in the wind and birds trill heartily from trees' branches. The nature that reflects us and we it, a constantly repeating imaginative act passing between us and the physical world, paradoxically 'unearthing' understandings even of ourselves.

To view the landscape alchemically as the *prima materia*, the starting stuff of imaginative work, is to see its symbolic possibilities as a raw material transmutable by the mind of the 'alchemist' walker into his or her gold. A tree their branching, the leaf litter their complexity. Then to understand the universe 'pantheistically', upholding Blake's belief that everything that lives is holy, is to embrace the earth and to begin to redress the unfortunate denigration of matter associated with the feminine. In calling for us to see the spirit alive in matter, she drives us on to celebrate and nurture our world with soaring thoughts and deeds to stroke and soothe her solid heart.

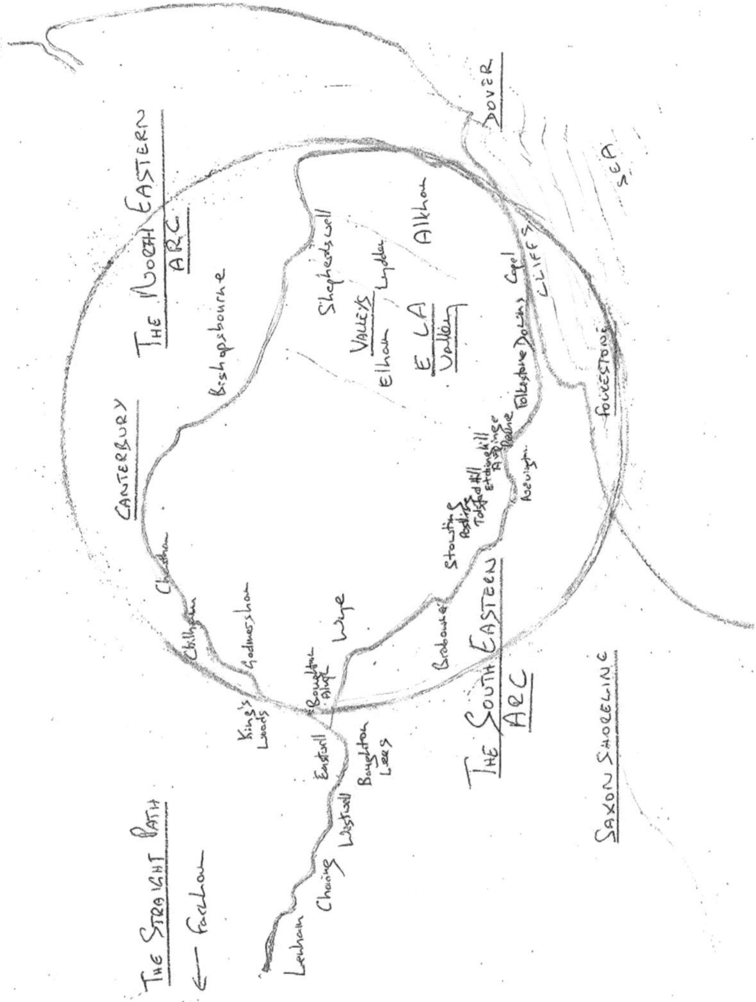

Map showing approximate Ring formed by southeast and northeast arc of North Downs' Way from Boughton Aluph to Dover, the places that have inspired this book.

April 2019 - March 2020

Arpinge Escarpment

April

Pillars Wood, Paddlesworth

Leaves haven't yet blotted out the spaces between trees so the stark woodland poised between winter's demise and spring's epiphany, is still fully open and light. Clear as glass, bird-song echoes through the empty spaces; air is now a balmy eighteen degrees after days of cold seemingly without end. Ground that will be relegated to summer's shadows in a month or two, laps up the sun's rays while it can, and there's an ease to walking; the once impossibly muddy wintery paths now dry and solid, starry white anemones on banks beside them harbingers for bluebells just appearing. In azure, cerrulean or cobalt they'll reach full spectacle soon along with all the sights, sounds and smells now abounding but specific to April's palpable sap rising. It is not the cruellest month. If anyone is enticed to take up the nourishing pen or paintbrush again in unison with April's swelling, it hardly makes them suffer. On the contrary.

In the fields outside the woods, lambs bleat a distant cry like the birds'. Nearby all is silent except for a sound that is a little creepy. A rustle, a creak, a scratch. Is somebody there? Sometimes Gurkhas with painted faces move stealthily and low over the ground of the forests' paths, rifles at the ready, looking sharply to left and right, but usually, thankfully, ignoring me. But no, no person or people ruffles through the crisp, dead leaves. It's the upper branches of these spindly, denuded trees scratching against each other, swaying in unison and connected by a breeze that makes the alarming sound, not falling debris; but also carries intimations of the wood-wide web; networks running through soil that allow the trees to communicate. Do they know I'm here? Is there something they'll help me say?

Though we know this scratching of branches is not the

trees talking—they have no control over the wind that rustles them—current studies show that trees do indeed have a language to communicate with each other.[2] Ethylene gas for example, dispersed into the air, warns other acacias nearby of leaf-consuming giraffes, electrical signals that move a third of an inch in a second.

Researchers have heard 'roots cracking', suggesting trees communicate through sound-waves[3], and the wood-wide web of underground fungi is known to enable trees formerly regarded as threats, competing for nourishment, to be, on the contrary, keeping others alive, sharing nutrients, co-operating in 'community'.

Fresh horizons of knowledge are opening, but very familiarly before me are the sinuous elephant-grey trunks of the trees stretched and shadowed by this newly warm and slightly hazy soft light. So too the pictures I am about to take of Dog cantering low upon the hard path between green bluebell fronds. I'll have to consider new ways of capturing the moment. Different seeings and sayings. But today there don't seem to be any and I'm in awe again, afresh, of all that is the same.

But why do I always photograph Dog when he's standing poised and proportionate against the backdrop of the illuminated trees with their long shadows and against the green leaves dotted with anemones? Where is the action, angle, movement? Present too I hope, but there's something about the beauty, the rippling slant of Dog fitting into the slant of shadow, which doesn't change for me; sleek, shiny Dog satisfying the same aesthetic as Black Beauty did for my inner little girl. And perhaps this enthrallment isn't so childish after all, but a valuable constant.

Horse, of course, is Dog. Compositions of the dark shade of him against landscape add intensity to other colours and their hues. Whether to the rape field behind, its

---

[2] Wohlleben, Peter, *The Hidden Life of Trees,* William Collins, 2017, Chp. Simard, S., *Finding the Mother Tree, Penguin, 2022*

[3] Ibid p. 13

furrows repeating impressive curves upwards between the yellow on the steep field, or to the bluebells of Reinden Wood, his blackness contributes three dimensional drama to the scene, his positioning dramatic scale to composition. Sharing something with Mark Rowlands[4] who found being around his wolf to be attracted by a beauty—art in its highest form—he couldn't emulate but nevertheless made him feel more alive, its presence always lifting his spirits, like my adorable wolfy dog, too.

Unassuming Pillars Wood just north of Paddlesworth is a quietly, nature-friendly walk place that I think of when I fancy that little release of earth smells during and after rain. Pheromones exude from a decomposing carpet of leaves, bouncy under foot, and here's the reminder of the complex simplicity of intertwined trees and rooty holloways. Emerging from these into flat fields often spread far with sheep, I sit and observe the swaying voluminous boughs of chestnut, hornbeam, oak and beech on a breezy autumn day, peregrines flapping their wings into the air, a buzzard or two hovering, overhead.

Paddlesworth is noted for its *Cat and Custard Pot* pub. Its Church at 600 feet above sea level, and 50 feet higher than Dover Hill, is made of Lenham Beds sandstone laid down when East Kent was submerged under sea in the late Miocene (5.3 million years ago) and early Pliocene period. Patches of its rusty brown sand can be seen scattered along the crest of escarpments and higher parts of the Downs. You wouldn't know you were high from Pillars Woods, but when you come south of Paddlesworth you can glimpse the sea glimmering far below.

---

[4] Rowlands, Mark, *The Philosopher and the Wolf*, Granta, 2008

Its promise enough of liquid worlds of aquamarine and gold. So only in my mind if I want to, can I raise its level, draw it up over me like a mantel so I'm covered with the enormity of aeons of changing landscapes and a picture of how it was all those millions of years ago.

Pillars Woods, Paddlesworth

Reinden Wood

Reinden Wood. Bluebells and fresh buds and Dog backlit by a late afternoon light. Several dogs barking at his passing translucence. A muscular rottweiler with foamy snarl, a couple of fluffy things that bark and bark their noise into the faded forest. A woman who ignores them like we do, says hello.

Part of a WW2 military village you can find remains of surface air raid shelters made of brick and concrete. Wooden structures were dismantled after the war, and there's evidence of the military still using it for training (East Kent Dry Training Area). Larches, a non-evergreen conifer (with cones) that drops its leaves, and Douglas firs with three-pronged cone scales, important habitat for woodland plants and butterflies, line our path, and sink deep into an interior we're forbidden to enter.

But the sound of fading barks still hangs in my mind's ear as if the forest has invisible walls marking the edge of a sound box. In it are stored echoes that float in and out of the butterflies and flowers that will come. Anemone, bluebell, ramson and celandine. Barks that have turned to shapes. Notes of music.

The Warren

May

Copt Point

I'm fortunate to have re-read Herman Hesse's *Siddharta*. He talks about a metaphorical river in our lives that bears us along. Source and mouth, waterfall and bend, current and sea, it is everywhere at the same time. Our past and future lives are separated in the present only by shadows, and these are without time. Time separates worlds that are really one, and herein is rooted our sorrow. How then be done with it?

By rummaging over the rocks around Copt Point. Standing back to convey the edge-ness of time and eternity that stretches backwards and forwards in the prescient air of this stimulating place, where everything that lives, it feels, is energy continually transforming.

Perhaps flights of nature will allow me a little flight of metaphysical indulgence, but how, in trying to describe the sensation of being here, where once we were joined to Europe? It's as if I'm caught between this energy's formlessness and formedness, in land or sea, or you or me. I feel myself to be living within the tension, which is palpable, of this specific time and place—between freedom and captivity, movement and stillness, ethereality and physicality—yet also able to seek the respite of timelessness and placelessness beyond it.

June

Elham Valley

I love the walk along Hall Down from North Elham with the valley below, but today we hope to walk up on to the other side to look across the valley back to Hall Down. Bullocks on the other side of a fence chase us, Dog pursues a badger unusual to see in daylight, and I must swim through tangled fronds of rape to follow the only path across the field.

Then at last we cross the road and enter at the base of Hall Down where the path couldn't be softer, safer or so luxuriously green. In fact it is so unsecular, so out of this world luxurious, that it may be just that. Another more translucent world which opposing the opacity of William Blake's 'fallen' nature appears almost diaphonous. That is how he envisioned nature to be before the Fall. Translucent all within.

Elham Valley

July

Pent Downs, Postling

This time we park so that we can enter the Pent Downs by the gate that cuts through the Downs on an open, springy, valley floor curving widely upwards to confront a scarp-flank marked by a chalk gash. Up and around again to the top whose long grasses are distinguished today by sharp sunlight that gets behind to pick out strands of Dog's black fur, too, as he surveys the scene, his scene, nose turned towards the wind, tail streamlining out behind; textures intertwining both in and out of my mind.

Pent Downs, Postling

August

'Coming home' - Along the River Stour from Fordwich

River Stour near Fordwich

Cluster-flying off branches of birch, grey-backed leaves rise and flicker from densities of nettle and fern like aspiring striplings. Rosebay willow-herb sprout pink-flowered, and willow fronds hang pendulous. Each intersperses with the other and all conspire to wrap the eye into a centre whose edge, it interprets, has formed a tunnel nestling around this meandering track.

The sultry day, jungle humid, is pendulous too, ponderous in a still air, thick and heavy, like these sinking willow branches into other denser foliage. Yet as this tropic humidity caresses my bare, brown arms and strokes my soul, what bliss it is when raindrops begin to fall gently, not yet cool but liquid compliment to the touch of warm air brushing over my now pampered skin.

Under the thick leaning trunk of a willow, Dog finds still pools to paddle and play in the river, but mostly the sides are too steep. The ripples he makes stretch out across the water, spreading under the bright green leaves of the willow that dangles and tickles the fragile water's surface, the membranes between things seeming minimal here, quivering and fluttering over all manner of organism, large, small or microscopic, in perfect balance visible and invisible, with everything else.

A jungle-bird coot hoots on a lake. An oar dips and more ripples stretch out across the water elsewhere. A motor burbles. Dog splashes. Often there is a dog as white as is black dog black in the distance in front of us, out of reach then out of sight. To our left, narrow passageways cut through thickets of bramble and fern opening out as we near the waters of Westbere Marshes.

A fisherman on an earthen jetty encased by tall reeds and bulrushes feeds peanut butter balls to tempt carp. Another fisherman on another such jetty jutting into the lake is playing music in his tent and we retreat before he knows we're there. And along one passage cutting through reeds, we come face to face with the whiter than white dog with his owner, and they who have eyed each other from a distance now play for a bit.

Returning, I come together in one swing. Body and mind. Not knowing quite at what point it is that a walk becomes more than itself, turning into a meditation and an inspiration, emanating from sights and sounds into a magic kingdom, coming to me only because I am alone. As I, as we, will all be when we die. A host of black butterflies take to the air. Dragonflies sparkle, teeming and teasing with spirit life.

And a man with a thick, silver mane like a lion's, who's waved to me from the *Ethelbert*, has now had to call out to another boat for a tow. His prow appears enmeshed in a bank of reeds, a family with children behind posts decorated with flowers can do nothing to help him get the motor going. It sparks then dies. The skipper of the other boat has been enmeshed, too.

I just saw him cutting out his engine to remove weeds from the propeller, but now he's tied *Ethelbert*'s rope to his boat and is pulling him back to his mooring, while Dog and I walk beside them, coming home this time. And another.

River Stour near Fordwich

September

Arpinge Range

It's not just the sight of these gently slithering coombes and scarps of hills that open up for ourselves the inner landscapes of our own minds, but also the feel of them. The wind that parts the grasses, rustles through my hair, caresses my cheeks and arms.

Despite arguments to the contrary, the strength of the sun of an Indian summer in autumn is never as high as the summer's. But these are just the speculations of a sun-worshipper whose summer-tide truly sparkles in veneration of the sun's tanning rays. Their effect in the deepening conker hues of her skin.

Arpinge Range

October

Denton Valley

Denton Valley

A straight track cuts through the green undulations of soft hill. A primal scream in a story issues from a woman, my friend, whose adored dog has its head clamped inside the jaws of a Japanese fighting dog: a true tale she told yesterday as we walked through Reinden Woods.

Another woman, another friend, howls for her aging daughter with a mental illness that prevents her from nurturing her own child. I was with her last night.

If we equated the scream with the track, we'd want to get off it. But if now it is speaking of extreme disquiet, at other times it speaks of order.

Although I am on the straight track it is muddy, so Dog and I are pleased to find places off it on the green fields, and there it feels that the howl at the impossibility of order, is less loud.

In the sweet dips and troughs of hills sliding up or down and away into clumps of trees whose leaves are turning yellow and brown, is release, like the magic of the mana personality suddenly surfacing. 'Where have you been?' I ask it. 'Where the power and wisdom?' The damp of the fields is squelchy underfoot and the puddles in the pebbled path too deep for shoes, but the air is mild and in its cocoon mixed with the smell of the earth, well-being arises.

Court at Street: The Holy Maid of Kent

Upon the startlingly green slopes of what was once the flank of a Saxon cliff with sea spreading out over what are now the flat lands of Romney Marshes, is a great brightness of sun, and it is absolutely still. So warm and still in fact, that though we are heading towards the end of October, I lie down, full body stretch on springy grass. I'm just outside Court at Street beside the flinty ruin of a chapel.

The earth feels its way into the small of my back and up my spine, holding me enriched in its firm presence. The wide girth of an oak tree around a little pond, presumably formed by the flow of the spring from under this higher part of chalk scarp, suggests it could have been here at the period of Elizabeth Barton, 'the Holy Maid of Kent'. Eerie the way this beautifully open vantage point paints that time as close to us now.

Elizabeth may have been the only woman to have had her decapitated head skewered on a pole and left on display for all to behold at London Bridge, but there was more to her than that. At this chapel beside a spring, once belonging to a hermit, she was miraculously cured of her derangements and illnesses, and here began receiving divine visions and the gift of prophecy.

People flocked to see her—I can imagine this empty place peopled. But her mission, 'brave for a woman', was to talk Henry VIII out of divorcing Catherine of Aragon (to marry throne-seeker Anne Boleyn), as God had forbidden it. When her prophecy that he would die within a month if he disobeyed never came to pass, Henry was at pains to show by her execution. Slippery Cromwell in praising Elizabeth for her good works had managed to get a long list of followers from her, leading also to the execution of Thomas Moore and the unleashing of a more thrusting Anglicanism against Catholicism.

This October has been particularly wet, but interspersed between the dull, overcast and windy have been three days of sunshine upon clear, horizontal landscapes. One in the Denton Valley, another on the marshes at Fairfield, and now here, with The Holy Maid of Kent where, as sharp and as wide as the place's horizons, arrows of an ancient presence fly, arching through the tensile mind.

I can imagine Elizabeth up here experiencing visions. The open magnificence of the place lends itself to those. And there's something pleasingly incongruous about this remote, tranquil, even transcendent place's connection with a pulse of power that once caused a paradigm shift in the country's direction, but that despite this violence a gentle landscape still prevails with an overriding ambience of peace and utter bliss.

Chapel ruins at Court at Street

Lydden Valley - Metaphor to Matter

For three days spreading across the end of September into October we're deluged by warm rain, and by the second of October a sun so bright and a sky so blue distract from the fact of definite rather than subtle change: an air distinct now with a bite anticipating winter.

The shadows are sharp, my thoughts less so. An excitement cuts through my mind, grateful. I've found work in the creative environment of an art school as a learning support assistant. Used to freelancing from home, I'll be unused to travelling to another building, and although that won't be incarceration, nor will I have the Downs to wander at will. How privileged I've been!

This is the walk I'm having after my first day of taking notes for an absent student, a time that has cut into the old structure of my day. Something about the continuing sharpness of the shadows is getting to me. I am cut also. We are cut. The shadows cut us so acutely from each other—others' uncaring cold like this new bright light, but as bright and light as my joy in being here parted from the shadow. Yet on a day like this, a little tree on these exquisitely sculptured hills reminds me of the singleness of my mother who painted isolated trees. Not lonely but free.

And in thinking of her I think matter/mater/mother. B has written to me about the mother's *animus* in shadow. That is Carl Jung's definition of an unconscious masculine in a woman as opposed to the *anima* which is the unconscious feminine inspiration in a man, although these days we need to see *anima* and *animus* as part of the human psyche beyond sexual identity. That in as much as *anima* doesn't belong exclusively in the unconscious of a man nor does *animus* in a woman.

I tell her about my mother, a strange early life with never a complaint then or now. Brought as an infant on a ship from India, with a nurse and a goat for milk, she'd come to live with her grandmother in Hove. My mother was separated from her parents for long periods as her mother had chosen to stay in India to supervise a philandering husband over being with her children. But when my mother's grandmother, who was looking after my mother and her sister in Hove, died, her mother came over to England to find a carer for the two girls. In a shopping queue she found a stranger to take them in—hardly a thing social services would condone now. And the money she paid the woman stranger went to her children rather than my mother and her sister.

With time and assurance from landscape, I've begun to overcome the sufferings and anxieties of (her) separations passed on. Cheerfull, intuitive, talented artist, my mother was also a qualified physiotherapist who didn't practice because of my father's larger income.

Baptised Catholic she integrated with Protestantism, while I, Protestant to begin with, was drawn to Catholicism later, for Marian reasons. It is a surprising reason as it is so paradoxically at odds with the shortcomings of a Catholicism that often denigrates the flesh and can deter us from looking at better and more uplifting significances. For the Marian belief that so inspired me was and is to be found in the Assumption where her body is exalted, and received, along with her soul, into heaven. With this, her physicality celebrated, representation once and for all is given to a divine feminine. And with that to matter/mater/mother too.

Talking my walk thoughts, the archetypal feminine, divine or otherwise, of which this Mary is one, stretches across cultures and myth in legend and belief. Sophia of the cabala as Wisdom, the Wisdom figure of the Wisdom literature in the Bible or Jerusalem in William Blake's Prophetic Works, to name but a few.

Elsewhere as positive soul companion she is *anima* in Jung, *emanation* (female counterpart to the psychological functions, *zoas*) in William Blake or *dakini* (female embodiments of enlightened energy) in Buddhism. If buried she needs to be brought into the light. Then Jung's broken individual becomes whole, Blake's Fallen zoas Unfallen and Buddhism's 'poisons' are turned to the Wisdom of the dakinis. Positive archetypes reinstated bring matter back to life, land itself now a living archetype, not separated by dualism's slicing of a 'superior' 'spirit' from an inferior 'matter' (as mentioned in the introduction) which has so denigrated the earth it depends on.

Lydden Valley, near Everden Cottage

This is a roundabout way of bringing me back to this landscape as matter/mater/mother, *anima*. In creating with 'landscape triggered prose' do I imagine I can put metaphor back into the material, imagination into place, bring the *animus* principle in woman/mother, *anima* in man, out of the sharp shadows filled with disquiet, into a pure line of beauty as in the undulations of these hills?

I dream I have a place at Cambridge University and my father is faintly pleased, but there's not much point really, I say, I've got a Phd already. Three tent tepee type structures that to me represent the masculine trinity sit on a round wooden table representing the feminine quarternity, at the right hand (intuitive) corner of our garden. If much of my mother's *animus* was in shadow—it wasn't encouraged to come out in the workplace where value, apart from motherhood, prevails—yet in her art it was. With this, and the singularity of a little tree reminding me of her, prompting these thoughts on mater/matter/mother, what a positive dichotomy she's left me. Thoughts coming from coombes that cushioned and cradled and carried them. From a father, a thinker, who mothered these too.

The Warren

The Warren is always extraordinary. It is an edge place funnel-of-breath. But that's only when it's windy. When placid and peaceful, the lid of funnel that seemed to have been created by the boundaries of the wind, is lifted. Before it was as if violent gusts had limited its vastness, directing space through a narrow tunnel, taking the breath away. But without the extreme movement of wind this open, central place opens and centralizes even further, dissipating its sense of place while grounding one in it, spreading its centredness outwards in a widening circle.

From the definite line on the edge of concrete the sea and sky beyond seem separated only by a crease with a boat dotted on to it. This is the horizon, a seam folded between one form of glass made of liquid and another of air, so smoothly do they seem to flow, one into the other, all a stupefying oneness.

The sound, though less dramatic than the crashing angry waves, is just as lively, but with a gentle lapping-ness that thuds a little then oozes away, melodically, swooshing-ly, slurping-ly, coming back for more so I am never alone and this is now the centre of the world, nothing happening anywhere else.

The Warren

November

Brabourne

Bright in Brabourne. Crisp with sunshine. New path patterns by-pass the house. Don't let the old ones persist with expectations of this or that. But don't say 'do-away.' Softly incisive they pathway through green grass, transform energy, convert with compassion and clarity not cold. Up over the brow and away. Traceable backwards to bygones converging just out of reach.

Brabourne Down

December

The Leas

Christmas. If on this special day people go about their ordinary lives, feasting, drinking, communing, they're also elevated by the ordinary having become exceptional, the transcendent, every-day, the physical they might fancy, imbued by something spiritual. Along the Leas, silhouettes in a living dream, those clambering at pains to say they're not religious, walk transfigured by a setting sun. They may even have sung *Hark the Herald Angels Sing,* the incarnate deity *Veiled in flesh, the Godhead see,* hearing without hearing about the Word, the god in themselves made flesh, the spirit that this event symbolizes come into their bodies.

The Leas, Folkestone

January 2020

Arpinge Range

Because I'm a ritual sunray-gatherer—particularly at this winter solstice time when the sun's early descent is so fiery and intense—my lone spirit plus Dog will long for the hills on New Year's Day, sunny of course, myself and my children able to raise our heads above the parapet of festive fugs. The coast is clear.

We'll turn away from the glistening sea to head inland to elevations west of the Folkestone Downs on the Arpinge Range near Peene Quarry or Etchinghill. For a while we'll walk and talk. Then from across the flow and glow of golden flanked Down, we'll be dazzled by an ever-changing veil of rose-tinted ambers and yellows that sweep across our vision, till the orb, departed behind Summerhouse and Tolsford Hills turns the once guilded grasses white and colourless in the not-yet-dark.

Raising our gaze to whisks of peach-pink ribboning the sky, we'll cherish the belief that all must be conceived of, if not done, on New Year's Day if they are to happen at all. And up here you can give it your best, letting words tumble, wishing for well-being everywhere. As we look down again we'll contemplate the sprouting sappiness of earth to be, and a pint of beer alongside a welcome at the Radnor Arms in Folkestone.

View over Brockmans Bushes

Etchinghill Scarp Sunshine

I'm an infant lying in a pram looking up at a blue sky through leafy branches. Dappled sunshine bursts in beams and twinkles through them. Ecstasy fills my being. Not everyone's memories of babyhood, if they have them at all, are as rapturous as this one of mine. But Carl's and Virginia's, my heroes, are remarkably similar.

C.G. Jung describes lying in a pram, in the shadow of a tree. It is a fine warm summer day, the sky is blue, the golden sunlight is darting through the green leaves. The hood of the pram has been left up, he has just awoken to the glorious day and its beauty, with an indescribable sense of well-being[5]. The sun glistens through the leaves and blossoms of bushes. 'Everything is wholly wonderful, colourful and splendid'[6].

Woolf also lying on a bed in the nursery in St. Ives

---

[5] Jung, C.G., 1963, *C.G. Jung, Memories, Dreams, Reflections,* Fontana Press, 1995, p. 21
[6] Ibid.

where her family holidayed, half asleep half awake, hears the waves break and splash over the beach behind a yellow blind. 'If life has a base that it stands upon, if it is a bowl that one fills and fills and fills—then my bowl without a doubt stands upon this memory' she'd said[7].

These early experiences of nature as numinous sunshine and reverie accompany us, muse and companion, throughout our lives. Green was backlit. Chlorophyll does turn sunlight into energy. Thus Woolf also had a sense of things we feel with great intensity being independent from our own minds, having a life of their own.

Creature backlit, Etchinghill Escarpment

[7]Woolf, *Virginia, Moments of Being,* 1976. Ed. Schulkind, J, Revised Lee, H. Pimlico, 2002, p.78).

Tracks Etchinghill Escarpment

Mental landscapes mirror nature's. Demise and infinity are in a grain of sand. Despite the threat of violence or abuse we conceive in the shadows of the wood, so our peaceful ecstatic experiences of nature default also to our early conception, to nourish and protect.

Majesty of sea

Short and pithy, rythmic and proseful. Thanks R. for what you call my artful piece for *The Guardian*. So why the weight of the worry, the wave on the wind? Because it's all here, below and within us, and twice today in this gusty tempest on top of the cliff, my home, I've been drawn to make a visual record, zooming lens into the fury of the waves so designer but unpassive-patterned. For the afternoon outing I've talked to Dog about where we should go on the Downs, but the driving rain pours down again, no big expedition possible. In between squalls we get out just to what is on our doorstep, just to what is on top then under the cliff, circling in our own land within the eye of the storm.

The weight, the worry, the wave, the wind all here. Not just the perpetual reminder that I have nowhere else to go but no need to—beauty in all weathers at its height right here—these forces real, not to be imagined or meditated away and no need to travel to find them. The weight and the worry, real too, even if they can be born off by wave and wind. And if we reverse it, the worry of the weight, the wind of the wave, it's just as true. Wave-weight, worry-wind.

The poisons of the dakini energies are true as well. Isolation and confusion. Anger, coldness, control. Arrogance, pride, insecurity. Craving, grasping, ache. Envy, ambition, haste. But these as represented by the elements air, water, earth and fire, can be transformed into the 'space' of all-encompassing wisdom, the 'water-clearness' of mirror-like wisdom, the 'earth' enriched presence of equanimity, the 'fire' energy of discernment or the enlightened activity of an all-accomplishing wisdom. But not yet.

Space is still without room. Water without hydration. Earth without solidity. Fire without light and air without passage. The fallen elements of Blake's zoas. All expressed today by the furious one, the rasping weight of the worry of the wind in the wave. The wrathful. The gusting howl around our eave this eve. The weight of poisons. The majesty and power.

And how melancholic in this howl is the sight of a man one loves, walking slowly, wrapped in weatherproof coat, stooped bent and low against the wind and rain.

February

The Sea

I stood waiting for my bus at a stop near the South Bank having just kissed my twenty-something daughter goodbye, hovering for a second over her soft cheeks, a sense of sweet-smell coming back. Time kind. Time it was when I'd never be without my baby, infant, then child. Each child. Time was, twenty years ago, not forgotten but moved on. Time was, when standing still had also moved away. Though pining in short measure, time drawing us so slowly and surreptitiously apart the separation that could never have been countenanced, invisible, as she, we, flower again, passing from one of life's stages to another. I going in, she coming out. Not without wanting, but because we're powerless on the inexorable river that wills it.

I get closer to the sea I look out upon. Its energy, crashing in, swirling round, winding out, is breath-taking. Objects, like rock, revealed by its sucking, tinkling leave-taking, stand out like memories before they are covered by the waters once more, and again and again.

March

Arpinge Range - March's march

Time as the barrier that curbs thought stops the swelling of a particular kind of life that's more organic than cerebral. That reaches up or down to us, or we to it, but abandons us when constricted by the edge lines of time that separate us, one event from another.

It's the flutter of wind on our cheek that inspires, a feeling of well-being deep in the chest that rallies, a spark of brain activity that makes sense, even momentarily, of the spaces and places in-between the time when we've an appointment to be in them. Was it 10.30 am or 3 pm?

Imbibing forms of nature fills lung's easier breath, melting the strictures of time's separating outline, slowly but simultaneously dissolving the matter it embellishes. Nature provokes the thought that is linked with feeling that swells and spreads beyond and above the finality of a day landmarked by time. The mildness of March.

Above and beside time's line wriggling across the Arpinge Range or through a marshy field at the base of the Saxon Shore line, clouds puff out, grasses burgeon lush. Though the marching path of 'doing' might cut through 'being' when we 'do' or when we 'go' (to work), bounteous being, these springy pastures, pushes back, keeping us bolstered, brave and bouncy.

Arpinge Escarpment

COVID-19

23rd March 2020: Lockdown.

Tolsford Hill, Arpinge escarpment, shoreline

Impossible to keep up. Far too alarming to look away. This was what writer Olivia Laing[8] exclaimed of world events.[9] From nuclear war to the Islamic State, the rise of the far right, Brexit, environmental disaster and now global pandemic 'the act of making sense' is continually frustrated within the twin forces of speed and instability.

Today, the twenty third of March, we are instructed to self-isolate. We might have felt isolation before from parents, siblings, children, friends, whoever, whatever, but not like this. Now is the seriousness of it. Or is it? Could self-isolation be a logical conclusion to the way we don't communicate anyway, as in Simon and Garfunkel's words, 'Fools, said I, you do not know, silence like a cancer grows'. Isolation, not only just being thrown upon us, but only now being confirmed as an always present.

Yet another reality is being confirmed, which pulls the broadest lie out of an imagined isolation. It's taken a virus—an attacker seeing no barriers of Brexit or immigrants or foreigners—to show or remind we're all connected anyway.

Another view of loneliness describes it as 'failed solitude'[10], i.e., we have failed to be complete in our solitariness. This appeals to me. Dog and I go up to Tolsford Hill, then the Arpinge escarpment where nature's shapes—the sea, the hill, the tree—furnish and fill the mind and I cannot feel alone even if I'd wanted to. 'The world has become lovelier,' also said Herman Hesse in

---

[8] Laing, Olivia, *To the River: A journey beneath the surface*, 2011, Canongate Books, amongst other

[9] *Guardian,* 21st March 2020

[10] Vincent, D., *A History of Solitude*, 2020

Wandering[11]. In reading his reflective mood, 'I am alone and I don't suffer from my loneliness', I'm reminded how well his words serve always, but particularly during lockdown.

Much credence has been given to 'community', but sometimes the peer group and its implicit pressures, like social medias, subsume the essence of the individual. If at our archetypically rhizomed roots we are all inextricably linked, it takes acknowledgement of the sacrosanct nature of each individual, fully fledged in independent thought, to be able to give their best shot to this dependency within our universal family so not to drown in a flood of collectivity.

But whether or not we're successful in our solitariness, the loneliness of being remains. The creations of the artist express our longing for connection, our craving for beauty, our attempt to overcome loneliness and alleviate meaninglessness and mortality. If metaphysically and existentially lockdown brings into cutting focus what has always been, practically it gives us a chance for creativity.

I'd disagree with a friend who claimed writing can only partly alleviate our loneliness. Often it encourages us to explore and go deeper into our relatedness. In the weaving of words to get at what we mean, we extend the possibility of communication with those who would best understand us, even as an ideal that falls short, even if we live as if on the edge of a breakthrough that never comes.

From where I am looking out at sea a sprinkling of people stroll along the shoreline but veer away from other couples or single people in a way that would have been rude when community was all. For a moment it looks noble. The individual given space. But this isn't extolling the individual's right to privacy, rather its threat to another's health.

If 'not touching' has become the outer sign of an distinctness always prevalent, it also warns of others as dangerous, exacerbates a fear of Other bordering on

---

[11] Hesse, H. *Wandering*, 1972, Farrar, Straus and Giroux

xenophobia if we're not careful.

25th March - Giddy Horn, Wye

While the virus rages I go up to Giddy Horn contemplating Hesse's tome. If one half of the wanderer's quest is adventure, he says, the other is an unconscious drive to transfigure and dissolve the 'erotic'. As a wanderer who develops feelings impossible to fulfil, he is, he admits, inclined to scatter lightly the love that might have belonged to a woman, rolling it gently out over small towns, mountains, lakes and valleys.

Yet, rather than marking the end of his love, his feelings for a young woman stimulate its awakening and beginning[12]. What we love is a symbol[13]. Every road leading the wanderer home[14].

The promontory which strikes out from the plateau of the North Downs east of Wye, one of several spurs reaching south like fingers from a stretching palm, is sunny today. Unlike the denuded-of-trees-sculptured-flanks of Pent Downs Postling or Arpinge further east, these are wooded with dense and secret forests lining the base then reaching up to their summits.

Coming through a last clump of trees, turning right into a field along the edge of Giddy Horn, I look up to the hill's horizon, surprised to see bare branches of two trees rising in the middle of the field when the thick woods are to my right. Suddenly these branches move and have big brown eyes.

They belong to a couple of roe deer bucks who aren't trees, staring startled at us before bounding away below the horizon, out of sight in half a second.

When I first came across this lush expanse of wooded scarp I'd not realized the dark blotch on the rising hill ahead of me had been a herd of deer until they ran off in a

---

[12] Ibid. p. 21
[13] Ibid. p. 6
[14] Ibid. p.15

cohesive scampering bound. Today after seeing the bucks we'd continued east around the curve of hills and looking down into impenetrable woods, spotted two small does who'd not noticed us to begin with.

Then they get a whiff of us and are off. Today I realise it's difficult to have the inspiring thoughts that filled Hesse's peregrinations. The blackness of death we're so bad at facing yet is confronting us so directly, hangs low in the stomach. And although these sudden apparitions of the natural appear almost supernatural, and so spellbound am I by the presence of these ephemeral creatures that I resolve to come back to these magical woods, I'm not joking when I talk of ill-ease in the stomach.

After seeing the roe deer bucks I'm literally gutted, a pain spreading all over my belly, nowhere near the heart, but in the gut, which, it is said, is seat of the second heart. My body's response is telling me not to be blase about Covid, which in reality is a shock for us all. Breaking out in rash outside, a pain inside, our bodies take the strain.

Yet when I make an effort to relax the pain decreases. I'm privileged to have an image—the grace of running deer in a natural world—to contradict the pandemic. Is the virus natural or human-made? I panic again. However liberated I am up here on Giddy Horn I'm also isolated. If I had a heart attack, even before I'd had a chance to contract the virus, nobody would know. Then what would Dog do with a dead human I wonder, imagining him running from this remote spot to find help but not knowing where.

26th March

Descending from the golden-grassed plateau to a delightful path through some sloping woods, thinking of deer, the mystery I'd love to see, I suddenly get a strong sense of 'presence' right here beside and around us. Dog lurches downwards towards something he's heard and a startled pheasant flies up squawking.

Then there's a rustle, a fluttering snapping of twigs

many times over that extends into a kind of wind. Unmistakably, though I can't see them, it must be deer. We round the end of the coombe and look down it. There they are, crossing over to the shelter of the next trees, looking anxiously back at us.

Now we've made it against all the odds of barbed-wire fences and locked gates, we look down into the thicket and spy the deer again, moving through tree trunks as dark brown as they, two turning to fix me in the eye before moving hurriedly off. Winding down the path to Giddy Horn's base a myriad of narrow paths trodden by deer hooves crisscross the wild garlic not yet in flower.

At the base of a promontory leading up another coombe a third sighting takes place. Two does with variegated coats, white and brown, stand glorious in full detail of sunlight, too tempting for Dog not to chase while they leap startled up into the air, easy over the fence and up again into the woods. Where were the antlered ones I wondered of the bucks as we drove home, the round red orb of sun bursting in my car-mirror.

27th March 20

We arrive at the eastern base of Giddy Horn after skirting along the side of the spur east of it, to see the group of does standing about nonchalantly in a paddock, unaware of us just for a few minutes.

A buzzard sits on the pole of a fence on the other side of the ripe stretch of green grass. Instead of flying away as we approach, it glides straight towards us, wings spread like cloaked arms raised in benediction, forging a passage in air over this enchanted plain.

If social distancing requires us to go inland/ inwards, what a time for the imagination. Exterior worlds turned inwards. Moving out of everyone's way it's now ok to embrace without hug-embracing our sad, lonely-bastard-ness, 'Space needed' being a legitimate slogan to strap to us as we move forward through the crowds.

APRIL 2020 — MARCH 2021

Brockman's Bushes from Peene

April

Chesterfield Wood, Pedlinge

Into a second month of lockdown and from Folkestone to Wye—as if heaven were made for one—I have the Downs to myself. All this is glorious countryside and just Dog and I, pleased in a way but asking, why? Taking the car out to walk locally isn't forbidden so it's surprising no-one else is exploring.

On the way to Chesterfield Wood, Pedlinge, I listen to a man on the radio talk about the joy of springtime birds with their increase in song thanks to the pandemic; the early swallows coming from countries we can no longer journey to. The buzzard mistaken for an eagle. Confined as we all are, these are the riches he has found, that have everything we need and more.

Time for a look-back, a re-order of a past. This is one of the perks of lockdown too. Today my head is full of characters from a diary I wrote between the ages of eleven and twenty-one, extraordinary to be in dialogue with strangers known so well fifty years ago. As nature brings out all feelings, today it brings out that sense of loss. Those who peopled my world no longer present to me. I have exorcised them before, gradually, and now I let them go again while also feeling they walk beside me still.

I park the car, not allowed at a car park these days, but it is pouring with rain, and my phone tells me without being prompted how many minutes of this are left. We can kill half of that time in the woods, I make the good decision. A canopy of oak, sycamore and beech in Chesterfield Wood protects us from the heaviest drops. Under our feet lies a carpet of late bluebells. We take little paths off the main one to see if any follow the stream and into Brockfield Park, also just to kill time. But mostly, at one with the soggy undergrowth, bright green shoots and birdsong delighting in the drip of leaves and lessening rain, this intensely secret place that I still cannot believe is unpeopled, ushers us in.

And no, the movement I see when I peer through the trees isn't a person but lower branches. Magicked into the squelch and the drip and the trill we find another path and another, and still the rain hasn't stopped but we're umbrella-ed from getting drenched by the tall oaks that strike postures around and above us looming with the assurance of bright green waterproof canopies between us and the heavens.

Today I have thought of the quirky, otherworldly representations of life by painter Carol Weight. At an art seminar online I had been envious of students' desires to create things out of household bits and pieces of bottle, plastic, metal, when I have no such ability, and can barely describe what is perfect here, and lovely, in the woods, from where I could go back refreshed.

I think of the thrill of the birdwatcher on the radio, being here with never a sign of anyone else. We don't go back yet and the rain subsiding as the prediction said it would, head off down an old familiar path towards Sandling Park. Between Chesterfield Wood and Black Hill we discover an unfamiliar route that skirts around the edge of a field.

By an opening into some more woodland Dog poses under a tree, his linear form echoing the position of a branch leaning out above him, as if this were just typical of his awareness of composition in landscape.

Chesterfield Woods

And now he's leading me to some water before only glimpsed through dense foliage but never reached. We are beside a lake! Smaller in scale than Hampstead Heath's Women's Pond and womanless, it has that same inviting, dip yourself into enticement and, belonging just to us in its mirror-like wisdom, pulls reflections of trees towards its centre in perfect un-stationary stillness. A transparent veil trembles over dark peaty depths, but not so dark you can't see the bits of last year's leaf and twig skim the surface, clouds floating above its floor's earth in reflection.

A puckering. A crease. A ruffle. Barely a ripple attaches itself to the membraned surface, and a flicker, a flutter in the mind responds to the ripple effect that sustains us whether we will or not.

Chesterfield Woods

The point about coming across a secret lake to hold—beyond the sighting of it—an image of a fluidity that won't be contained but remains in memory like a shot imprinted on photographic paper, truer than you know. I'd not been thinking of my haven, the charming lake in Pond Field on the Heath Extension from long ago, but there it was, its concentrically layered capillary waves skipping ever wider from the central place where my pebble had once landed to ripple water outwards for its own sake, no matter that resemblance to the effects of lives.

Giddy Horn, Wye

Today, 4th April, my birthday. The deer are visible across the field on the edges of the woods where I park below Giddy Horn. They're in the same spot when we return.

The lockdown that 'sets us apart' also saves us from our isolation, for we're not alone in being isolated and contrary to our solitude is driven home our connectedness. Beyond the arguments between race, class or religion that have divided, profligate, humbling death comes to all regardless who they are. By death as the reason for birth we might be persuaded not to chase after passing things. By Covid's total disregard for politics we should call for ceasefires, right now, everywhere in the world. Turn our economics around so we value our carers instead of our profiteers.

Up here on Giddy Horn the world has become lovelier as it had for Herman Hesse when alone (see p.52). 'I am alone and don't suffer from my loneliness. I don't want life to be any other than what it is. I am ready to let myself be baked in the sun until I am done. I am eager to ripen. I am ready to die, ready to be born again.' [15]

An undiscriminating virus shows us our equality with each other and belittles our petty conflicts. It also shows us appreciation by absence, even if that's a pint of real ale we dream of in the welcoming glow of a pub that's shut down. Walking up along a narrow chalk path six days later that carves its way through scrub and low tree on the coombe's eastern scarp wall, I look up through dark branches and trunks to where daylight shines at the top of the hill and can just make out, in the same brush-stroked, undetailed brown as the tree-trunks' burnt sienna, the horizontal body and vertical legs of a couple of deer.

Dog has been poised focused too but on another sound I couldn't hear. Then he's off and the deer career wildly away from him across the top and down some where I can't follow. But as I move on and look up again I spot two ears, a face and neck of a doe that got left behind and is looking down at us, Dog now having returned after a breathless chase.

---

[15] Hesse, H. *Wandering,* 1972, Farrar, Straus and Giroux. p.17

Ascending Giddy Horn

'It's ok', I say to her as I hang on to a substitute-for-forgotten-lead pink scarf that I've lassoed around his neck, 'he won't bother you again'. A little further on there's a cracking of twigs. The couple of does that got separated from the rest run back through the trees towards the coombe and their reunion.

Beachborough

Looking down from Brockman's Bushes on Etchinghill Scarp is a coombe flanked by steep terracetted scarps opening on to flat pasture I'd not explored. The Drake Brockmans who owned this estate went to Victoria, Australia, whose National Gallery has a picture of the 19th century estate when its pond, rotunda and lake were a part of the house, and Summerhouse Hill really had a summer or swearing house as it was called, for the lord of this manor to come and let off steam.

Summerhouse Hill, Beachborolugh Park

We can also imagine the land formation going back further, forces of rivers ripping across the earth to forge deep coombes and sides, Summerhouse Hill eventually separated from the bulk of these Downs by weathering. To enter Beachborough's coombe is a different world to standing on the edge of Tolsford Hill looking down, but no less impressive with its graceful open sweeps and manicured curves half-human half-nature formed.

Now I've been here four times. The first I parked on the road to the south, headed towards Summerhouse Hill then round the elevated base of Tolsford. The second an earlier stop on this same road, simply walking round the base of Summerhouse Hill. The third determined to find the pond and rotunda, which I discover parting branches, so to speak, lying in a deeply wooded recess.

The fourth, today, I reported a fire in the undergrowth with my new smart phone. It looked as if some hay beside a ten-foot stack of logs had combusted, but apparently it was being managed. To find I had readily available internet to trace who was responsible for the land, would, for better or worse, extend the possibilities of looking up distracting as well as relevant things whilst walking, if I chose, from now on.

I returned to the part of the pond by the bricks that might have formed the base of the rotunda and thought of this pond peopled by women in elegant dresses from the picture in Australia's National Gallery, the cliffs of France in the background, the general sociability of then an eerie contrast to its deserted privacy of now. Its covering up by untended shrubs and unintended passages of time.

There's a claim that the same amount of water exists in the universe at any one time, it just changes from one form to another. In the mood for recurring spectres I transposed my wonderings to people. Perhaps there were always the same amount of souls, but they kept on taking different bodies. The spooking didn't stop at the pond.

As I'd been walking along the northerly side of Summerhouse Hill I'd seen a couple with their dog descending, almost reaching me but not quite. Then as I rounded the southeastern side I glanced sideways to see a dark figure and a dog approaching, but hesitantly. The next time I looked he/she wasn't there. Then looking back at Summerhouse Hill the couple who I'd seen descending were at the top of it again. It was easy in this landscape to believe in time warps.

Reverie stirred by bright spring sunshine had cast dramatic shadowy abstracts over the simple, shapely slopes with an almost hallucinatory effect. Figures foreshortened in the far and near. People you could imagine going round and round the cone in trapped time. Slopes rearing strikingly from open, intangible and endless, distant ground, close and touchable.

And if souls are fluid like water, a little bubbling stream seems to have taken shape for Dog who bounds to get to it through spring grasses as strikingly green as is the slope striking in softness, splashes in and out, careers off wildly, and does it again not phantom fey but recurringly.

Summerhouse Hill, Beachborough Park

May

Everden, Lydden Valley

In *Wandering*, Hesse described how he sought the alpine canton of Ticino in Switzerland after the War to lift and refresh his soul. We might be 'caged', unable to go to Switzerland during lockdown, but we've not come through a war and can find uplift by looking at landscape. Yesterday's Arpinge Range stretching out from Peene offered health restoring space in lieu of valleys of alpine soaring Europe. Today I look south over the sea. Gaze north at the possibility of going inland.

I'm thinking of the quadrangle of West Hougham and Old Hawkinge, a smaller square with Flegis Court and Hawkinge Hall about three miles away, but they confuse me with their similarities. It doesn't matter, they're lovely spots from where I'm standing, but I reject both in favour of Lydden valley behind Everden Cottage, my best 'sand dune' area to which we're now bound.

The valley is eerily quiet but having come from Hesse's book where all roads lead home I consider all valleys leading along the base of a long spur might do that too. In a zen way if you like, home always now. Nature burgeons around this coombe which directs itself flatly northeast like a flowing river. Sometimes it is scratchy and chaotic with scroggie shrubs but today it's flat and smoothly ploughed, Dog transfixed to a spot over dusty pink mud and flint whose significance only he can know.

Because Hesse has slipped with such synchronicity into thoughts befitting lockdown, I wonder and wander along with him in *Wandering*. How we needn't bemoan what we did or didn't become; to be what we're not would do violence to who we are, increase the world's pain; a society of individuals only half aware of itself leading to further tyrannies and oppressions.

Nomads can take their hearts with them over the mountains, the largesse of its gently pulsing love like pantheism, in all things. Or agape, universal and transcendent. They can leave their ego-centred Eros's behind, their craving for grandeur and fame, and without being fixed to one place carry God, peace and home within.

Lockdown has honed such thoughts like blades of a two-edged sword, for this goodness or love aren't always available. If the self-avoiding routines that have been taken away will save or sink us, bringing us face to face with a self we've not seen for a while, that might not bring salvation at all. For lockdown is rife with psychosis and mental breakdown, the result partly perhaps of what we've ignored, reminding that although 'going solo' could put us in touch with 'who we are', that's not always so straight forward. But now we have a small chance. That helped by nature to make that flight of personal imagination possible, the instinctive heart thus exposed will know the way.

Arpinge Range

They are unflinching and solid these spurs who spur me on like encouraging friends, but I'd be mistaken if I based my survival on undeterred resilience. Covid has brought us sharply up against the fact of our own deaths, but despite this we bring out tactics to avoid and fight it. Like William Blake's character Tharmas representing instinct, we lift our head from alchemy's allegorical clay and will life rather than death. And when recovering from illness we behave like heroes who've conquered mortality forgetting that one day it will get us—and are unable to look forward to that unless we believe this life to be prequel to another.

If Hesse saw wandering to dissolve the erotic, Antal Szerb in *Journey by Moonlight* viewed dying as an erotic act[16] with fear having sexuality at its base, a form of desire. But Covid rather than gratifying a last sensual blast seems to have induced in us a sense of being grateful, just to be alive. A healthy by-product that sees us behaving more respectfully in creative and everyday ways, as if, as Potawatomi botanist and author, Robin Wall Kimmerer has said, there were a 'contagion of gratitude', running in the veins of a deep time.[17]

This reminds me of a time in the early seventies when I woke alone in a friend's apartment in Chelsea on New Year's day, feeling extraordinarily elated and grateful to be alive as I walked out into the sharp air of the streets. Though I can't remember my friend at all, we were in our mid-teens, I can still breathe in those joyful moments. Of the sun on the material of the pavements, rays bursting through splindly branches of a city tree, Joni Mitchell's song on my lips:

---

[16] Szerb, A., *Journey by Moonlight,* Pushkin Press, 2001 (1937 first published), p. 156

[17] Kimmerer, R.W., *Braiding Sweetgrass, Indigenous Wisdom, Scientific Knowledge and the Teachings of Plant*s, Penguin, 2020. Also Guardian article, 2020.

Woke up, it was a Chelsea morning
And the first thing that I saw
Was the sun through yellow curtain
And a rainbow on the wall
Blue, red, green and gold to welcome you
Crimson crystal beads to beckon...

Our gratitude, like deep time, is here to be tapped into. It could be in a conversation with the natural world. A landscape that resonates within. This 'landscape triggered prose'. Similarly, Kimmerer in a Guardian interview defines her writing, 'as an act of reciprocity with the living land.' [18] I look again at the strength of these impressive spurs on the tip of deep time's iceberg, providers of a feast of nature's morsels stirring language to flight, salting and nourishing the expectant mind.

Arpinge Escarpment

[18] *Guardian*, 2020

June

Elham - Trees

Before we know it June has topped the spring, silently, unobtrusively, pushing up the sap, swelling out the green. The holm oak that was sculpted in its relative nakedness (though evergreen its leaves thinned in winter) is more wonderful still: decked suddenly in swaying weights of foliage, and I have found it again, huge and spreading, on the Leas. Its roots dig into the very foundation of the mud-covered cliff. How far do they descend, does the cliff hold the tree or the roots the cliff?

Holm Oak, Leas West

The tree that is a loner, Hesse continues in *Wandering,* is not like a lonely person who's hidden away, rather a great, solitary man—let us say woman too—such as Beethoven, Neitzsche, also Angelou or Woolf, struggling to fulfil their own laws. To build up a form that represents them. Listening to trees doesn't mean we want to be a tree, only that we can be at home in ourselves and when anxious our path is leading away from mother and home be reassured, once again, that home is nowhere unless within us, every path leading there.

Although Hesse claims nothing is holier than a beautiful strong tree, with God not its forbears or children within it, a man who's been planting trees in the sandbanks of the Brahmaputra all his life views them as his sons and daughters that speak through their leaves. The leaves converse with the wind and ask for water. Nature is God, trees nature, and in as much as the Hesse metaphor can be useful, we know, in the light of authors Susan Simard's and Peter Wohlleben's[19] researches at least, that far from being loners trees have very refined life-saving and social connections with each other.

But we are still in the grips of the pandemic as well as the murder of George Floyd, and however many homes or trees we experience, we are both afraid and raging. In thrall to strange juxtapositions, our spirits open to cerulean skies and grasses dappled with scarlets and yellows only to get dashed again by isolation and repetitive hatreds. The pandemic taking us to the extreme of what was already present.

Yet now as I drive home from a hospital in Canterbury, I'm overjoyed to have been granted a further lease of life by investigations that have shown the lump on my breast to be a cyst. More time to submerge myself in the abundance of over-spilling greens that line the road, deciding that Hall Down in North Elham is the best place Dog and I should go to lap this up, where this time last year we experienced a similar burgeoning green.

The Down doesn't disappoint on this slightly sultry pre-storm afternoon, strips of fields climbing up on the other side of the valley bordering on blue and yellow green.

---

[19] Simard, S., *Finding the Mother* Tree, Penguin, 2022
Wohlleben, P., *The Hidden Life of Trees,* William Collins, 2017

Bursting bright viridescents on oak, ash and hornbeam swish gentle and heavy in a caressing wind, not pernicious today, gnarled trunks appearing from the ground as extensions of their earth-sunk roots.

Having walked the hawthorn-lined valley, we turn around to avoid the cows and return upon the diagonal slopes of the scarps that cast their well-defined edges as satisfactorily as the golden-rule composition of a masterpiece. The grass may not be as high as last year and it is pleasantly not as hot, but the more sombre colours are balm and full of hope against what a hospital visit might have revealed.

Many of the trees aren't solitary but gathered together like humans—like the cheerful nurses I saw today—laughing and chatting down the corridors, eyes smiling above the masks, each coming from their individual stem. They tower and shake so majestically, I could well believe they were glad to be here for another season... (if it weren't for the risk, the pay, the exhaustion, etc....)

A huge black flint shaped like a foot wrapped round with a line of white chalk seems to leap out at me, smaller than my other friends the sculptured hills or foliaged trees, it beckons to be taken home for a doorstop. I'm thinking how easily places in landscape and shapes in the world give form to the mythic: islands to paradise, hills to hope, trees to strength, cliffs to endings, wide fields of crop to openness and wind in these leaves to telling me such things about a stone that has become a talisman. Flights of fancy grounded in flights of nature flavouring the imagination.

Alkham Valley

Ripe valleys and fulsome trees make for a perfect June in Alkham Valley. Still reading *Wandering*—by now accepting it's my 'wandering'—I'm feeling alive to the nuances of air, cloud and tones of colour, wondering like Hesse, do we read an image of our own inner life in the sky or is the cloudy sky mirrored in our souls?[20] For if the tree swell in my pictures is definitely there, so is my mood which has been created by it.

Perhaps it's because the pandemic refutes our immortality that I like what Hesse has reminded me of. Not to want to become what I am not. See the long distances once travelled as part of the 'soul'—no need to journey to make them real[21]. Glimpse nirvana and the death of contradictions—no need to impress[22]. With 'home' thus in

---

[20] Hesse, H. *Wandering*, 1972, Farrar, Straus and Giroux, p.100
[21] Ibid., p. 105
[22] Ibid., p. 107

the heart, wisdoms on the doorstep, I put the black flint that I've carried back as a weight, on to the faulty dustbin lid in the kitchen.

Brabourne Downs

But that presupposes we're able to see 'the world in a grain of sand' when at moments of being incarcerated we might not be able to. And an obsession such as mine with 'looking out' might be antidote to the narrowness of 'inward looking', the terror of being trapped, denied freedom (as distinct from introspective 'looking in'). But not in the case of Brabourne Downs where these vistas are a joy in their own right, total and complete, feeding an introspection as positive and appropriate by-product of social distancing during the pandemic.

For several mornings I've awoken with an image of a particular holloway that leads from a small lane on the North Downs Way up towards its higher aspect on Brabourne Downs. Today, when the wind is rattling the scaffolding that encases our home, we will take this windbreaker of a route away from it for our afternoon constitution. Not really thinking of views or looking out at all, I wonder if this lane might be able to tell me why it was beckoning in my half-waking, half sleeping dream.

A new look out answers that. Along its rocky southwestern path lined by what had once been thick, impenetrable foliage, are now knarled and swaying trunks and branches rubbing together in the wind, eerily squeaking, denuded. No foliage. The trees and shrubs have been taken back to give a new opening right out over the plains towards the sea, as at Brabourne Downs just along from here.

After we've gallivanted and lain down in the lovely long grasses under some spreading oaks and I am ready to turn back, the second 'look out' is demanded by Dog. He urges me on until we're up the road to the top of Brabourne Downs overlooking...everything. He's right we shouldn't have turned back without witnessing that.

'Looking out' we might also be looking up, down, above, below, over, under, through or around. What makes a difference is the decision to do so. 'Looking from' is the word that sits on my lips the following morning when I wake, as if comfortably from a white cottage at the base of a quiet valley, perception growing from me.

Towards Brabourne Downs

July

Asholt Woods, Newington – 'July Eye'

Fields transformed by purple Yorkshire fog flowers, dense tufted meadow foxtail, wood rush, cocksfoot and sedge. From brevity of spring to bursting July full to the eye, path and forest floor brim, obscured by grasses and leaf-bloated branches on darkening trees. The route through field and forest floor has multiplied its sights, sounds and scents, unrecognisable as the place it was in January. Into banks combining columbine, cow parsley and eggs and bacon cavort marble whites and dark evening brown butterflies. Blackbirds sing, chaffinch and chiffchaff beside the privet flower's strong perfume. Richnesses balance so there aren't two sides of the path, but layers. Layer built upon layer upon layer of scent and sound and sight.

Arpinge Range - #MeToo

It was another one of those walks that took me out without having to think where to, and there we were, on the Downs, around my favourite part. A bright sun on the flank, no shadow on this July day but a sense of dark somewhere in the fractured, misunderstood light. A recollection of unease.

I didn't make this landscape but here it is. The rule of silence that has been passed from generation to generation like a hot coal not to be mentioned has been stern. It has turned us inside out. We are encouraged then discouraged to share our vicissitudes. It has made us feel bad even about feeling bad. To deny what has been denied us. Strange that in a culture whose bedrock is individualism we should not easily be able to say: Me. That is until the encouragement of MeToo. But even now there is the betrayal after the rape that mustn't be mentioned. A trauma normalised, a slow plummeting death, if we're not careful, to mind and body.

And here is the other landscape. I know these spurs so well and yet we are traversing the slope of one on the many terracetted tracks—step-like, regularly spaced ridges running down the hillside—along the second spur I haven't done before. It is very open and precipitous but not so sheer I can't be comforted by the cushioning clumps of long summer grasses that dip more gently into the green coombe yet are still plunging enough to be one of the more dramatic spectacles of the North Downs.

I look out at these monumental formations and don't have to pretend that what I feel bad about is not just the pandemic. But there's no one else here, only the earth, to feel bad too. No brothers, sisters, friends.

I marvel in a perverse way that we can be so isolated from those once deemed close. This place and our positions sublime and lonely: the lonely sublime. But as such, here counters any shadow that would seek disharmonious, disease to splinter the light on these massive, solid, heavy hills. Old friends by now.

It could be ankle-twisting but it's still possible to walk along at any level of many terracettes to meet a more established path that leads across to the flank on the opposite side. Upfront flanks that glow brave and honest far above the silence that besets us all.

Arpinge Escarpment

August

Dymchurch, Arpinge Range, Paddlesworth

We look back at the Downs from Dymchurch. Mount the scarps around Arpinge. Look over France from a high golden-harvested field in the bounteous heat of Paddlesworth, the scent of cut hay, its sharp ends protruding from a ground that crumbles in some places and is rock hard in others. From dusty detail to abstract we take in both particulars and outspread patterns. Even Dog seems to cast his eye over them, the smells that must strike him most, reaching my senses a little too, feeding in the light that bores through leaves' stomata holes to turn carbon dioxide to oxygen, through gaps in the fronds, through susurrating motion of branches.

A man told me he didn't know what to do with nature when he was living on the edge of landscape. I thought it's rather what it does with you than you with it. David on the other hand had made his exquisite breakfast patterned with luscious fruits whose flavours burst again and again into the dulled of taste overnight mouth. Strawberries, pears, blueberries, bananas, grapes sliced and laid out neatly in star, sun or face shapes ready to be eaten.

Arpinge Escarpment

September

A Folkestone Night Garden

Dog who normally loves to visit a person who adores him, was for some reason reticent to go down the narrow side passage to the garden towards her. But here was her luscious paean to nature in a little corner, filled with green leaves and stems as thick as the balmy autumn air odoriferous with earth and ripening fruits. The elevated flutter of a single silver birch rose over us in a warm and gentle breeze, the perfect pre-winter, Covid evening for the four of us gathered here, to sit out. Though Dog beginning to recover his equilibrium from a bout also of trembling caused by the letting off of caps we couldn't hear, retired more happily into the furthest end of the summer house.

He wasn't the only one who'd had the shakes. K had a disorientating disease that affected her balance, unpredictably, and sometimes when she was crossing the road. My son had had a similar affliction, labyrinthitis, brought on by a fairground ride. I'd talked with K about this often and asked her now if the best levels of medication had been found to control it.

Hurtful perhaps to those of us who'd considered ourselves caring friends, she'd answered that only her family and loved ones would be interested in knowing, she didn't want to bore us, so instead we talked about the tragedy of funding being cut for the arts. But the conversation—or was it just in my head—seemed to take on a garrulous turn, everyone competing to eulogize over the last best performance of this or that they'd seen, theatre, concert or gig. The eating places, the pubs, the architecture. Fair enough, we were brimming over with the freshness of what'd been denied as we were coming out of lockdown.

Only yesterday I slipped in we'd seen a live performance of classical music. On a lawn on a clifftop overlooking a sea pinkening in the setting sun. Under more susurrating trees, this time sycamores, the crimson twilight behind them turning branches into silhouettes, the notes of flute and violin weaving sublimely in time with the slightest of sways from filigree boughs, some held there in serenely waving clasps, others rising for a while to disperse into endless space.

The conversation was getting louder. Going into a blur. Rising to a crescendo in my head. This was not music, nor an argument, but a jangling, noisy monologue from a woman opposite that I could feel entering my stomach, twisting something inside it around, setting off that pain which though in an unspecific area was acute in an unknown everywhere like my first attack of it up on Giddy Horn when the pandemic was first announced.

Now it was my turn not to want to bore anyone about the contorting pains in my gut, but even if I was leaving them mystified and startled all I could do was flee, muttering apologies and thanks for the truly delectable food as I ran down that now dark, post-crepuscular side alley, Dog glued to my heels, suddenly neither of us even Rousseau creatures in and out of fronds anymore.

Rivers

My father stands to the left of the frame, the side representing the rational, my mother in the right-hand upper distance, the side of creativity. Here is the river, says my father as he points down to the left. Blake's Water of the River of Life, I think.

I'm looking up at a three-story house. It has a slightly shabby glass-covered porch overhanging the river. There's not much in the way of open views, but there's the river. And then the house starts moving like a ship. We are floating down the river and I'm not altogether at ease with this. In fact it's alarming, and I wonder who's responsible for this if it isn't God.

These last two were a dream. That we are standing on the precipitous promontory of Symons Yat rock looking down at the River Wye meandering before us, down and under the immediate yellow leaves of an autumnal tree, is not. Away from the Ring of Downs I'm not away from waterways that run through land as imagination through us. On these banks of the River Wye, above Tintern Abbey, Wordsworth wrote the words,

> I have felt a presence that disturbs me with the joy of elevated thoughts, a sense sublime of something far more deeply interfused, whose dwelling is the light of setting suns, and the round ocean, and the living air, and the blue sky, and in the mind of man...

The next morning, 9.49am, we are standing beside the Severn at Newnham amongst a group of waiting others checking their watches. The Bore is already late. And I can't imagine how it could fill this open stretch of water so very wide and shallow.

But suddenly it's there, a single wave, white curling then furrowed, the tidal water-arch of the Bore flowing in, rolling out a continuous furl, while from the land the opposite is happening. Water is flowing outwards towards the sea. Marked by little jaunty waves, the conflict of upstream meeting downstream sees the inland rushing tide locking horns with the outwards flowing, then held there, dancing, while on each side these two directions sidle around one another, one trying to get in, the other out.

The following morning we go to spot the Bore from Minsterworth Church. Bore in Scandinavian or Icelandic we learn means 'bara', a tidewave, a swell, a billow or a surge; a turning tide that has been trapped by narrowing and shallowing going inland, a constricted river tapering into a funnel. The Severn Estuary has the third highest tidal range in the world after the Bay of Fundy in North America and Ungava Bay in Canada... the tides are largest when the sun and moon are in line with the earth... so are linked to spheres of further away.

The Bore from here is narrower than at Newnham and

doesn't come as one singular wave, but nor is it a ceaseless repetition like the tide onto the seashore. It swells in four or five singular rolling ripples that billow then subside like an inflated then deflated balloon turning into a trickle.

Every day of living by the sea at home we witness a wave far wider, as wide as the entire coastline whose land receives its continuously ebbing and flowing wide-tide. The fascination with the Bore might have something to do with this channelling precision of its wave in contrast to the sea's, its tide more driven, narrowed and compressed. Its focus more singular.

The River Severn

October

Giddy Horn near Wye

As soon as we get out of the car at the base of Giddy Horn where the trees are turning orange, I am whispering to Dog instead of talking, and as we ascend up past thickets and through an avenue of trees to the top our silence is complete, if such a thing can be called of the whispering breeze in the leaves and a crow's alerting cackle overhead. We do not want to disturb the deer. Dog is glancing from side to side, sniffing the air, peering down through trees then up into the branches. He's anticipating their twig break, though it's us now that's making them, and I realise he doesn't know where the deer are though their odour is strong enough for me to smell too. A bright October sunshine throws highlights on to the perfect elegance of the trees, the silence of our stealth seeming to reach into the heart of the earth for a slow but eternal moment as we sense the interweaving of deep dark tree roots beneath us.

Once into the plateau of Giddy Horn we skirt along the edge of the forest still peering into the trees, but each time Dog scuttles about in his excited sheep-dog way and peers into doorways of light between the trees, never do I see the deer that he has sensed. Never mind, the silence and expectancy induced in us is the next best thing to a sighting.

But now we've broken over the fence into the dense woodland floor of leaf, twig and branch and I'm making my way down its steep slope into the brightly lit green of the coombe floor, I have reason to put Dog back on to the lead. There, just past the blackest of shadows from the trees, in the brightest of valley greens, sits a stag, looking at us, his antlers perfectly symmetrical. We sit down too on a tussock and watch him as he watches us, does grazing beside him. It is only when we get up, as we have to a few minutes later, that they all leap up too and bound away.

Placidus, who was out hunting him. Coming to a high rock the hart had asked why he sought to hurt him, Jesus Christ who had formed heaven and earth, made light to increase and divided it from darkness... and Placidus falling down on the spot—converted to Christianity to became Eustace. And despite the trials he faced—as depicted of his harrowed life in a wall painting in Canterbury Cathedral nearby—remained resolute in his faith.

Vale with stag at the base of Giddy Horn

The Leas

High-pitched low tide, short white waves trickle-roaring in, scuttling over bare rocks on a south-westerly, ripping up the cliff into sycamore and holm oak shiver-shaking their myriad boughs, striking through lone walkers and runners with and without dogs straddling the warm, grey air.

I am a lone walker, too, caught up in the wind's frenetic, invigorating dance, shouted at by the waves that tear up from below, yelled at by the trees that spill out from canopies' heights in voluminous leaf-filled wobbles and from out their ancient stillness, am a barely discernible flutter in their long-time breeze.

The Leas, Folkestone

November

West Wood Trees

I've been reading through some Jungian material for my brother written by his deceased friend Steve. Although I say he understands Jung's unconscious as different from Freud's—in that it adds the archetypes and mystery where Freud doesn't—he sometimes misses the point either by over-simplifying (in seeing it as no more than fairytale or

Father Christmas) or over-thinking it.

Contrary to what Steve suggests, Jung would have found it ok to view the collective unconscious as metaphor — a huge ocean perhaps with the ego as a pinprick (humans in their little boats) upon it. Or the vast interconnected and communal root system of a forest feeding separate, individual trees.

Now here we are in West Wood squelching over peaty mud, orange and yellow leaves glowing underfoot despite the grey sky. Seeming to hold it all together the immovable woody roots of several trees carpet the path like step scaffolding to stop us slipping, just a suggestion of what forms an enormous network of roots and fungi, new mycorrhizal knowledge informing us, flowing who knows how wide and deep below us.

West Wood, Stone Street

Godmersham

I'd wanted to walk in a circle up from Court Lodge Farm, Godmersham, along the edge of King's Wood on the North Downs Way to Godmersham Park house that belonged to Jane Austen's brother and is depicted on a 2017 £10 note, but this part of the North Downs isn't so simple.

The huge estates around here are unforthcoming with paths for common folk from Folkestone. But spotting one track on the map encouraged me to walk along a Private Road as the only way to get to it. Still no footpath sign, but we ascended anyway overlooking an old red-bricked wall curling upwards through autumnally denuding beech trees, their leaves still glowing golden under our feet, as well as pheasants squawking up from grassy banks as our footsteps passed nearby. Several tree house constructions looked down at us from the beech branches as I felt uncomfortable about the possibility of trespassing.

A high barbed-wire gate along a fence at the end of this track with its side facing away from us saying Private Keep Out, confirmed that feeling again, so I was almost relieved to see a small man in shorts and summer tea-shirt clambering up the steep incline towards us, obviously a walker not a farm manager, bewildered too about where he was and very hot. The fence was too wide for either of us to cross—easiest for distancing though we'd managed a conversation along the lines of hoping the Democrats would come through (it was US election day 2020)—but he'd parked his car in Godmersham, where mine was, and although I was trespassing and he wasn't, his walk was going to take him a longer way round.

If I descended the steep hill through the trees that he'd just climbed up he assured me I'd reach the North Downs Way that led along the side of King's Wood. But there wasn't time now it was getting dark and these beeches had provided enough solace for one winter afternoon, so instead we walked back the way we'd come, only deviating at the last minute, right up through an opening to brightness. Not expecting any reward yet here we'd got heights as well as trees to lighten our spooky-wooded, dark spirits, and today out of the darkness that was Trump had come to pass I heard, what we'd barely dared hope. The election of Joe Biden!

We had a new view now over the Great Stour valley, more undulations and glimpses of the river, small hamlets, flooded fields and lakes, hills and valleys towards Broughton Aluph and Wye where the Downs flattened. The turfy, bouncey grasses sloped down away from us as we continued along our elevated way, elated with this beauty like a re-turn to attitudes of Obama.

So it didn't matter when a little jeepy vehicle came roaring towards us, the driver though startling at first, perfectly pleasant, saying this large estate, unlike most, had no footpaths. Unfortunately. His boss had told him to come up to investigate the person he'd seen on the mound. I apologized, un-obsequiously, knowing this was a scene seen with eyes, set into the mind. No amount of boundary patrollers could take that away.

December

8th December first day vaccine administered to over 80s, home care workers and NHS

Etchinghill Escarpment - Dakini Mary

In correspondence with diaries I'm reading from childhood I dream I'm trying on a little girl dress in front of my friend—for the healing to work. Five tubes, amphoules, phials, fingers of a hand are needed. But they are also the five dakinis (female embodiments of enlightened energy) that I practiced yesterday on the heights of Etchinghill overlooking the sea, France and scarps: the four elements, water, earth, fire and air, with the fifth thrown in too. That is the ether in terms of Blake's four zoas (Jung's four psychological functions). Or space, same thing, as added to the other four dakinis, the whole which makes up the physicality of Mary.

Theology shows Mary's physicality to be Earth. She represents the Creation as opposed to the threefold masculine Creator of Father, Son and Holy Spirit. Matter of the tangible earth rather than the spirit of the intellectual sky, she is most urgently in need of protection and veneration against the 'progress' that desecrates Her and Her world. That undermines and undervalues carers in favour of consumers, the very workers and nurses even for whom the first vaccinations are being rolled out now so they can attend to the lives of others.

Chalk Dreams

The Warren, Folkestone

Buoyed up by dreams we lie on a bed of chalk that breathes both water and air. A dun of tiny sea-creature coccoliths millions of years ago have fed on limestone's minerals, got calcium carbonate to make their skeletons and shells, been crushed to form a limestone seabed, then been pushed up from the sea floor towards the sky. From mineral to animal to rock. We are not only lying on a landscape that remembers much but stretching back tells a story of being at the bottom of the sea. Loose and not as hard as granite, chalk is light and breathing, letting air and water in and out of itself. The water that comes and goes through this soft, white and porous carbonate rock, is held and then not held, passing out purified to leave the chalk dry.

I consider the microscopic creatures whose skeletons and shells forming white porous mountains in the sea got pushed up in the Paleocene epoch—some sixty-six to fifty-six million years ago—by tectonic plates shifting in a massive global upheaval. They were squeezed into a ridge from southern England across the Channel to Calais and rose with the same tectonic plates that formed the Himalayas some sixty-six million years ago (the Alps are older at 770 million years ago), then got flooded about eight thousand years ago. And if I'm wildly out as I grapple with these time expanses impossible to comprehend, it doesn't matter to geology.

Still:

Chalk is a miracle. Among geologies, it is a Zen master. Chalk doesn't grip, it holds on loosely. Chalk breathes in water and air, purifying and sanctifying as it does. The chalk that comprises so much of Southern England tells a long geological history of life in the ocean[23].

I dream the art students I support colour dresses, dense hanging strings beaded with chalk/rock, but when I take one student's home to wash, all its colours come out. Not knowing what to do I tell her. She is upset to lose her beautiful design, and also it will be expensive to re-do, as I tell her she must, though I will pay for it. Then, I find, the dress hasn't lost its colour after all. How could it in fact, it is made with rock when I thought it had been chalk, which might run when washed. I'll tell her I made a mistake, and chalk is rock anyway.

My own ambivalence about handling material which sometimes fills me with hesitation and anxiety, even though I enjoy texture and the feeling of things, may have been coming into play here, also how I chose university academia in the steps of my father's emphasis on mind instead of staying at less cerebral art school. Yet still words became my images to paint and play with and perhaps this dream is telling me something about chalk in my life. That although porous, allowing flow, is as resilient as rock.

---

[23] Hopper, J., *The Old Weird Albion,* Penned in the Margins, 2017

Dreams open to individual interpretation, like pain, belong to each of us alone but unlike an external stab to the flesh come from the inside, and unlike pain don't have to wound unless there's something we've kept down, not allowed through, kept silent and in the dark. When allowed to rise up through a loosely threaded skein, the meaning of a dream, or even just its presence, can absolve and set us free. Nor are they restricted to night.

The liquid unconscious of dreams brings sustenance and rich inspiration to the diurnal soul, too, a guiding companion to the day as water seeping through chalk filters upwards through spaces in our solid skin-covered consciousness.

During this pandemic the common casual conversation doesn't take place between people with the same regularity it was accustomed to. In lockdowns the presence of people we'd taken for granted, always all around us, sharing the everyday, is absent. But they come to life when we think of them, speak on the phone, have a zoom call, or go for an arranged walk. There's our memories of them too.

In my dreams they're there. Often people I haven't thought about for a while. Friends and strangers frequent a remembered unconscious and here at least is the bustle and shindig we're denied now. In the world of dreams, the warmth of loved ones and companions surrounds me on a morning when I wake, so here I'll stay. Forgive me if I look a little far-away and dreamy if at last we're ever able to resume everyday communication.

January 2021

Etchinghill scarp – 'Suspended'

On the top of Etchinghill's scarp, the horizon of ever increasing and decreasing hillocks and tumuli sit on a flat that spins with three-hundred-and-sixty degree outlook. This afternoon the line is compressed, squashed like a broad ribbon within a grey sky pulled down and a brown earth pushed up, bright and dark light balancing chiaroscuro. We might be trapped here were it not for the dashing flash of dying evening sun that strikes out like arrows under heavy, sombre clouds, thinly butter-knifing its spreading.

View from Etchinghil escarpment

Beauty feels to be hanging here, bright mixed with heavy ominous, incoherent only in the sense it's trying to say something inexpressible. Like a cloud that has no need of raining is this fluent, fluid beauty suspended without words, its speechlessness dizzying, intoxicating. And if you try to fix the band of horizon in your mind's eye the world seems to tip, first this way, then that. Unless you head to the neat clump, which is Brockman's Bushes where the band is now a straight horizon against stanchions. The wintery verticality of beeches that holds up the sky.

Brockman's Bushes, Etchinghill escarpment

Reinden Woods, The Leas, The Warren

7th January 2021. The earth is fallow. Over a thousand people have died from Covid (by the 20th it is over 1,800). Trump supporters have stormed Congress.

Nothing much moves or furnishes the bare trunks in Reinden Woods but underneath the ground seethes. New growth if we've the will to look, pushes up between parted leaves like pushing out the hours of daylight discernibly on the increase.

Reinden Woods

At midwinter, 21st December, the sunset on the Leas was at 15.49. Now, the day after twelfth night, it is 16.06. Seventeen minutes at this time of year makes a difference.

Sunset on the Leas

On the Warren a couple of days later, where despite the cold the sun was bright and the top of the cliffs were shrouded in a clinging wormlike cloud under an azure hue of blue, I didn't even think of the accumulation of fear and slime and horror in our human world.

Here the air was crisp, the wrapping cloud embraced the white cliffs as if they were snowy Alps, the name Little Switzerland for part of this area seeming appropriate, taking our minds on holiday for a while as we drift up and down the hillocks where the highland cattle—which keep the ground foliage down during summer but churn up the mud in winter—aren't grazing at the moment.

The bright green succulent leaves on the forest floor, antidote to our grey January, speak of a garden of Eden. A waking dream in contrast to conscious nightmares goings on; an exquisite, Italianate place we've come to live in rich with texture like a tapestry in flower.

The Warren

February

Denton to Wootton

I'm sure Raynor Winn of *The Salt Path* and *The Wild Silence* fame has already had it suggested that with her name she couldn't fail. Yet before she attained her lifetime's dream her writings were turned down many times. Now with publication, her beautiful language and imagery strung together with a compelling emotional thread takes us on a journey with people as remote from us as Adam who we suddenly care about.

I'm on a holloway leading up the hill from Denton to Wootton. Leaf on wintery leaf my footsteps kick up the serotonin in the soil. Our friends and relatives I repetitively contemplate fall off like these leaves from their branches, but they are still there, carpeting the ground of our being, the networks beneath us holding us together.

And yet I reflect a little sadly, this analogy is often betrayed. Raynor is alive to the network with the man she loves, but she has made her journey alone; the network that connects humans involving capitalism and having a roof over our head having been shown to be at best tenuous.

We are the human leaf litter. Human humus. Biological matter. And as humans we bury as well as build, bodies return to dust, inhumed, made humble even. Leaves both fallen and plateaued hold us as if we were on a plate, simultaneously let down then held up. Same, same, but different. And always but especially now these analogies of connectedness are important for us to sing about at this extreme time of our non-physical, non-hugging, non-meeting, social-distanced connection.

The wind today is taking breaths, fluttering hedges as tremulously as butterflies on the sides of the track. Between each sigh a silence, both as regular as lull and beat, lull and beat, moments of the stillness swooped up into a whipped dessert of movement finely tuned with sound before subsiding altogether into a vacated bowl, a breathless vacuum.

Further up the passage the moulded leaves are replaced by unadulterated mud, my energy taken by hopping from one side of the path to the other, to avoid the central quagmire mostly submerged in rainwater, and trying to keep upright. Then down a much-welcomed lane however muddy on the surface—tarmac underneath the sludge keeps the feet secure—to another holloway, minimally less treacherous than the first, and with open aspects over fields and pheasant habitats happily punctuated for Dog by little white fluffy balls of rabbits' tails' hopping and skipping away from him.

We round back more lanes via Wootton church. First snowdrops are peeping out from behind some gravestones. The deep dark firs and peaty coloured soil smelling of damp and serotonin accompanies our downhill stride as the view of Denton Valley opens up before us, bringing to mind yesterday's Alkham Valley and the holloway leading from the stables at Mount Ararat. We walk to savour these blessed places not introspectively but taken out of ourselves, extrospectively. In a dream between sleeping and waking a few days later, a disk as round as the sun, made of a texture of layered leaves, leaf-litter, and surrounded by a couple of outer rings, throbs slowly up and down, the earth our breathing plate.

The Leas

I can't recall when I last saw snow on the Leas or crunched gleefully through the crisp combination of that with underlying grass like crushed glass seeped into sponge. Crisp too the sky, deep dark clouds circled sharply by light, the sun shooting blinding expanses of wide and startling brightness off the sea. In other places outside this display, the light is grey but a jocular movement of prancing white horses on its surface dance incongruous against the static white snow.

Snow on the Leas

I'm reading of another, Icelandic, landscape too, of volcanic ash and lava, deserts of shale and spiking rocks[24]. A wild place where you can look into the fury of the earth's moving centre, oozing and splattering out, underground rivers flowing and spouting, the schism of tectonic plates dividing the moving ground. Raynor Winn describes the earth as if it were gathering itself in preparation for going about its business totally unbothered by humanity—like a muddy wet dog shaking itself.

Yes the dog wriggles and shakes unbothered, drops of water flying in all directions, and in both landscapes you can feel the force of this nature unfettered by humanity. But also, as Raynor points out, it and we will be bothered. Rivers flow beneath the melting ice-fields and greenhouse gases poised in a sea one third of which acts as sink for CO2, are ready to set hazardous methane free into the atmosphere.

I imagine this sea in front of me today to be as dramatic as these Icelandic seas. I mull over earth science trying to make it simple. Carbon dioxide giving life as extremely as it

[24] Winn, R., *The Wild Silence,* Random House, 2020

takes it away. In out. We needing the warmth but not to burn in it, getting the fragile balance right between the life-giving and the poisonous qualities of carbon dioxide. The Kali-esque balance of taker also giver of life.

I marvel at the basic biology lesson, plants breathing in carbon dioxide and sending it out as oxygen for us to breathe in. We breathing it out as carbon dioxide for plants to use again. Carbon dioxide forming a protective layer over the earth to stop the heat it got from the sun escaping. Photosynthesis transforming light's energy into food. What bothers me is not being able to see the carbon dioxide of which so much is spoken.

We know we need heat, especially as when last night, at -2, our central heating broke down. Luckily I'd got a fever from my Covid jab to keep me a little warm. But with this protection I look forward to being able stand next to people, unknown for almost a year, without feeling I could pass on the virus.

I contemplate the chalk of which the Leas is made, nature-writer Robert MacFarlane's 'liveliest of rocks', the limestone of which it is part, just one phase in a dynamic earth cycle that does a dance of life and death in deep time. I repeat what I said in Chalk Dreams. Coccoliths have fed on the minerals of limestone to get the calcium carbonate to make their skeletons and shells which later get crushed to form the seabed of limestone pushed up into rock. From mineral to animal to rock.

In his recent book's bid to save the planet, even Bill Gates' statistics are helpful. Hydrogen fuelling transport would curb emissions by 30%, but it is the steel and cement industries that cause most emissions, transport, surprisingly, including air travel, only amounting to something like 16%. Cows farting 4%. The limestone on which I sit, he explains, has to be burnt to get the calcium needed for his much-loved cement. Yet when we do that we get equal measures of carbon dioxide, so it's how to recycle it that becomes our challenge.

Saltwood Castle

It might always have been dark here where the assassins who made their plans to kill Beckett met, or where the walls were responsible for keeping Chaucer a prisoner. There's speculation that when England's most popular writer just vanished around 1400, it was the 'thought police'—as incongruously as if the Permissive Sixties had been pivoted into Stalin's Russia—who had 'dispatched' him. When Henry IV usurped Richard II's throne in 1399 it was one of the darkest, because hidden, moments in English history, historian and comedian Terry Jones describes. After thirty years of intellectual freedom when anything could be thought or written, the country was overturned overnight. Straight-jacketed, intellectually, in a way that had never before been equalled.

These curtailments, happening in other countries, aren't impossible to imagine in our own I think as I walk under Old Man's beard shadowing a view into the impenetrable castle where peacocks wander and Kenneth Clark of *Civilization* repute once lived.

Saltwood Castle

It is muddy in the extreme as we turn west to follow the side of a field, its banks saturated to swamp. After a few undulations over this pretty but squelching green, we are at a stream's bed around which it is almost impossible to keep upright until getting foothold on to a cropped heathland, far more reliable to the step, which inclines steeply north up a gorse-covered scarp. So steeply in fact that foothold is challenged again, but Dog looking back worriedly to see if I'm making it, isn't disappointed. We're at the top with tremendous panoramas back towards the Castle but also over the Tolsford Hill and Brockman's Bushes shapes of the North Downs.

We scuttle along the top overlooking the gorse, which this February is not yet in yellow flower, and see right over to the curve of St. Mary's Bay and beyond. But trying to get into the next field in order to strike out to the road that will lead back to a holloway taking us in a round, proves too difficult for Dog. There's only a narrow space between the top of fencing and barbed wire. His distressed whine tells me it wouldn't be fair to push it. Also a couple of frisky horses look too interested in our arrival.

So we roll down the sheep-sheared stubble of this land flank to the bottom, hoping to find a route back, but knowing if we get lost, we could make the steep ascent again and retrace our path. What had promised to be an open, mind-expanding exercise was beginning to be fraught with little darknesses.

While I beseeched Becket and Chaucer to lessen the hauntings of assassins, disappeared authors, peoples' freedoms and human rights, it wasn't looking good. Fields were turning to swamps again, the narrow sheep track fading. These hauntings were not unfamiliar to us today, I thought, noticing tyre marks in the track's grit, subsumed by the deepest sliding soil.

Follow it we must, and hey, it opens up into an idyllic valley shrouded by banks that look beautiful now but will be perfect in spring. Marsh reeds shoot up below them, and there in the centre a babbling brook, much to Dog's exuberance.

I'm not sure there'll be an opening in the direction I know we should return, so many fences and gates have been determinedly locked, but because the bog is too sinky to go north we follow the brook south, round and back. And here, oh I of little faith, is the right path. I recognise a leafy glade and see that I'm walking the other way back through it. Reversing other times.

From a magic valley we emerge to diss the darkness and fear and doubt—be gone!—and despite the sign I now see behind me saying No Footpath we've just enjoyed the perfect, pastoral scene for lovers and naturalists not killers or kidnappers. The goodness and wonder of water washing up from wet land's valleys. The heart escaping atrocity transformed by landscape.

Saltwood Castle grounds

March

The Warren, Arpinge Range, Etchinghill

A year now of distancing, it's our memories of each other, more solid than the ghostly replications of ourselves, that we converse and interact with in the absence of present physicality. We replay the people we know as bodies in our recollections of them, small conversations and moments expanding with significance.

The Warren

Of the friends I find in the landscape around they are always the cradling bay of the Warren or the bolstering spurs of the Arpinge Range in a late sun.

The Arpinge range

But in this Etchinghill picture below you can see shadows of Anna and I giving up our separation, real people together at last, not ghosts who don't have shadows.

Etchinghill escarpment

Saxon Shoreline

From the Holy Maid of Kent's one time chapel described in October 2019 I wondered which way to wander. Sheep could be one way, people pottering in their farmhouse garden another. But today both were to my west, so going south down the springy March-time slope towards the sea way off in the distance, and then to swing east, would seem the best option.

I'd not properly considered how coming to the Saxon Shoreline implied I'd be walking on the once seabed. How wide is this liminal place that seems to go on forever, my eyes fastened by an elastic band to the horizon, stretching them out, letting them in without pinging, like the tides themselves but with no delineated suggestion of where water might have lapped at its own shore.

Would it have been directly below the steepest cliff-like scarp or lower down where the descending and ascending gradient was gradual to where it gently joins the plain? Would I have been gasping for air here, at the bottom of the sea, or would that still be below me? If I am below the water-surface, I am still high, a view stretching away to where the sea now begins at St. Mary's Bay. And if I am very high upon this playground, I am also very low as I look up to the cliff starting just behind the chapel and spring at the steep side's base.

The air today is motionless and grey. The magic of this place often lies in its stillness. No wonder Elizabeth had her visions here, filling it and being filled. Any of us might in this 'thin place' between worlds, but not be so brave we'd challenge a tyrannical king and risk the taking off of our heads.

Ruins of Elizabeth Barton's chapel, Court at Street

And if I'm at the bottom of the sea I'm also on this bouncy spongy earth, the tussocks of grass beckoning to a warm spring. It will bind us, when we lie on its earth, to the sounds and sights of sap rising under rushing clouds. To call of lark and branches bursting with twinkles of white May. It is a buoying up place, soft and sliding. But today because there are no leaves on the trees to hide me, I feel exposed to any viewer, albeit from only the couple of houses nearby.

And if I'd been here somewhere between 18,000 and 6,000 years ago might I have seen the sea rushing up towards me as one more glacier melted somewhere not so far away? Or am I already in the sea as it drains away speeded up like the water from the bed of the Red Sea for Moses, relieved to find myself sitting and bouncing on turf-moss, bedstraw, arrowgrass and sedge, no need to cross out from here, this blissful bedrock?

Sea

At last we are talking to people. Do we sound coarse or superfluous against the sea, which has been pooled beside us all this lockdown as the continuous harbinger of our continued silencings and distancings? A soft rose-coloured misty pink dissolves the horizon coating sea and sky so they are alike, and then it is dark, stars dropleting out from the no-longer penetrable black.

On one of the first evenings of socialising outside we are a little self-conscious. Had we spoken too little or too much, born down too heavy over one thing and not enough over another, been too kind or too harsh, spoken of one person but not the other? These are the questions asked by our lack of confidence, our new anxieties unused to speech and social etiquette. The distancing is broken for us to wonder, have we let someone down, portrayed or betrayed them falsely or frivolously? Can our conversation be overheard?

Still, we are held fast by the presence of undying tides, and barely moving we remember the spaces we have found and exalt them. Turning from our pedometers to our stellariums we share with our friends the wonder of the stars we cannot reach and thoughts on dark matter that pass through us without touching.

Conclusion

Nature as panacea, physical and mental, has sustained us during the dark months of pandemic lockdown, so if we've been left a little weaker, shaky and traumatized both personally and collectively, perhaps we've also been strengthened in ways not easy to measure.

I'm hoping the challenge mentioned in my introduction—to the patriarchal order that has sought mastery over nature, a masculine 'spirit' superior to feminine 'matter' and our consequent plundering of Mother Earth, resulting in climate change—has perhaps been realized a little more. That's the value of 'being' over 'having' or 'doing'. The consolation nature brings to body, mind and soul, which is the main thrust of the book, depends on upholding this challenge. Our impatience and domination hasn't led to a better life on earth.

Covid is partly a respiratory condition. So too is climate change. Hearts and lungs, separated from heads as it were, have been thrown into our melting pot of vaulting con-

Sea and home

sumerism, but as we throttle and choke the earth, thought without heart, taking without giving, she retaliates with floods, fires, storms and droughts. With her outer skin desecrated by deforestation, habitats of her creatures lost, she is only attempting to right the displacements which have unbalanced her. And us. But by matter's reflex for living, a force which doesn't lie down, the impulse to dominate is shown to be vincible after all. A boiling cauldron seethes. Into it has been whipped a vicious cycle of infection and destabilized weather—not stirred by witches.

That spell cast by humankind in an ambitious tongue earth couldn't understand and bred by an ignorance that ignored her (are ignorance and ignore related?) was blind to her magic, bypassing the fact that earth was already replete. And though our imaginations in which nature is both mind and matter may seem inadequate to counter calamities that need practical solutions, they are not too small in helping us tune into this bigger and enchanted picture, find tools and templates in nature for overcoming dualism.

In flights of nature we can feel landscapes that resonate within us. Looking out over earth and sea, on shapes dimly perceived in mist or sharply in sunshine—twisting branches, swelling hills—our inner worlds vibrate with the perception of physical things, the visible world reflecting our spirits as do our spirits the visible, the designs in our natural minds duplicating the earth's patterns. Even the cycle of entropy if we listen turns in on itself to bring order as an ever-repeating energy.

The pages of this book end with March 2021, but they herald an April when the first full moon Sunday after the spring solstice which is always Easter, is for the first time in my life, also my birthday. Last April we were only a week into lockdown. Now I am blessed with my children all together at last. Now we can celebrate. Ponder symbols of physical and spiritual saps dying and rising in a dance that combines mind and matter in whatever pagan or resurrected bodies we care to imagine.

About the Author

Dr Maryanne Grant Traylen is a scholar of the work of William Blake and C.G. Jung, looking particularly at traditions such as Platonism, Gnosticism or alchemy that informed them both, as well as comparing the coming together of their opposites. She was founding editor of *Transitions,* a series of four annual journals, and *Stella Maris,* 'Marion themes explored', for the Society of Psychotherapy and Healing, as well as writer of articles and book reviews concerning the unification of science with religion for local and national newspapers.

Publisher and freelance editor she is now a writer living in Folkestone, southeast Kent, England, with the sea and Downs right on her doorstep.. She has scoured its shores and countryside on walks with her dog most days for the last thirteen years. So she knows it, one might say, like the back of her hand, and indeed has seen the eastern ring of the North Downs Way as a healing Jungian mandala, uniting the arc that stretches through Canterbury to Dover in the north with the other stretching through the Folkestone Downs to Dover in the south, in a personal touching of the landscape.

Author of *A Dog on the Downs* and *Ring of Downs* her other publications include *Climbing Sea, Sure Line Poems, Sea Saw Sea* and *Twenty Stories* all inspired by where she lives. As well as having taken literary tours for Pavement Pounders Community Interest Company in London, bringing the streets to life through its artists and writers who lived there, and assisting in the recording Folkestone's oral histories, she is Geopark Ambassador for Kent Downs National Landscape. Her walks concentrate on a geopoetics where landscape inspires language. In that the hills and coasts provide inspirational possibilities and reflections for writing prose and poetry her focus is on the Blakean slant of upholding matter as alive with spirit. She has two further books in the pipeline. *Light of Land* and *Ways with Waters*. Please visit **subbstack.com/@languageoflandscape**

Bibliography

Allione, T., Wisdom Rising, Journey into the Mandala of the Empowered Feminine, Enliven Books, 2018

Andrews, K., *Wanderers, A History of Women Walking*, Reaktion Books Ltd., 2020

Ansell, N., *The Last Wilderness*, Tinder Press, 2018

Conrad, J., *Chance,* Ed Martin Ray, Oxford World's Classics 2008, first published 1914

Conrad, J. *The Heart of Darkness,* 1973, Penguin Books, and the Penguin Essential edition, 2012

Crane, N., *The Making of the British Landscape,* Weidenfeld and Nicholson, 2017

Deakin, R., Wildwood: A Journey Through Trees, Penguin, 2008

Farley, P. and Symmons Roberts, M., *Edgelands: Journeys into England's True Wilderness*, Vintage, 2012

Garner, A., *Thursbitch,* Vintage, 2004

Hamilton, D., *Wild Ruins,* Dave Hamilton, 2015

Harris, P., The White Cliffs of Dover, Amberley, 2013

Harris, P., *Folkestone A History and Celebration* The Francis Frith Collection, 2004

Hawkes, J., *A Land,* Beacon Books 2001, first published 1951

Herbstein, D., *The North Downs Way*, 1982

Hewson, D., *Native Rites*, HarperCollins, 2000

Hopper, J., *The Old Weird Albion,* Penned in the Margins, 2017

Jones, P. Owen, *Pathlands,* Rider, 2015

Kingsnorth, P., *Beast,* Faber, 2016

Kinsky, E., *River,* Fitzcarraldo Editions, 2017

Laing, O., *To the River,* Canongate, 2012

Liptrot, A., *The Outrun,* Canongate, 2016

London, J., The Call of the Wild, White Fang and Other Stories, OUP, 2009

Mabey, R., *A Brush with Nature,* BBC Books, 2010

Manley, D., *The Walker's Anthology,* Trailblazer Publications 2013

Macdonald, H., *H is for Hawk*, Vintage, 2014

Macdonald, H.,*Vesper Flights,* Vintage, 2020

MacFarlane, R., *The Wild Places,* Granta, 2007

MacFarlane, R., Donwood, S., & Richards, D., *Holloway,* Faber & Faber, 2014

MacFarlane, R., *Landmarks,* Hamish Hamilton, 2015

MacFarlane, R., *Underland,* Penguin, 2020

Marsden, P., The Summer Isles; A Voyage of the Imagination, Granta 2020

Maugham, S., *Don Fernando,* Vintage, 2000, London (first published in 1935)

Nevill, A., *The Story of Folkestone,* Antony Rowe, 2009

Morris, M., Ed., *Women Travellers,* Virago, !996

Papadimitriou, N., *Scarp,* Sceptre, 2013

Parker, J., *Britannia Obscura,* Vintage, 2014

Pavord, A., *Landskipping*, Bloomsbury, 2017

Powers, R., *The Overstory,* Vintage, 2018

Rowlands, M., The Philosopher and the Wolf, Granta, 2008

Self, W., *Psychogeography,* Bloomsbury Publishing, 2007

Sethi, A., *I Belong Here,* Bloomsbury, 2021

Shepherd, N., *The Living Mountain,* Canongate Books 2011, 1977

Shepherd, N., *In the Cairngarms,* Galileo 2014, first published The Moray Press 1934

Simard, S., Finding the Mother Tree, Uncovering the Wisdom and Intelligence of the Forest, Penguin, 2022

Stamp, D. *A Glossary of Geographical Terms,* William Clowes and sons, 1966

Taylor, A., *Folkestone Through Time,* Amberley, 2009

Thubron, C., *To a Mountain in Tibet,* Vintage, 2012

Tuson, D., *The Kent Downs,* Tempus, 2007

Van der Post, L., *A Story like the Wind,* Penguin, 1977

Van der Post, L., *A Far-Off Place,* Penguin, 1977

Winn, R., *The Salt Path,* Penguin, 2018

Winn, R., *The Wild Silence,* Random House, 2020

Woolf, V., *Flush: A Biography,* Indo European Publishing , 2011

Yarham, R., *How to Read the Landscape,* Bloomsbury, 2010

www.ingramcontent.com/pod-product-compliance
Ingram Content Group UK Ltd.
Pitfield, Milton Keynes, MK11 3LW, UK
UKHW020106170326
469067UK00001B/163

9 798896 561057